VERONICA L. VANHOOSE

BENEATH THE SHADOWS

Illuminating the Path Out of Depression

This book was professionally typeset on Reedsy.
Find out more at reedsy.com

Contents

About The Author   v

My Journey From Darkness To Light   vii

CHAPTER 1: INTRODUCTION   1

Purpose of the book   2

Overview of Depression and it's Prevalence   2

CHAPTER 2: UNVEILING THE SHADOWS   5

Understanding the Root Causes   6

Impact of Stigmas and Misconceptions   10

CHAPTER 3: ILLUMINATING SIGHTS   15

Unveiling Emotional Depths   15

Recognizing the Need for Change   20

CHAPTER 4: REDISCOVERING JOY   22

Therapeutic Approaches   23

Medication and Psychopharmacology   33

Brain Stimulation Therapy   35

Practical Steps for Daily Well-being   40

CHAPTER 5: PERSONAL NARRATIVES OF HOPE   47

Real-life Experiences of Overcoming Depression   47

Lessons Gained from Personal Journeys   57

CHAPTER 6: TOOLS FOR TRANSFORMATION   58

Practical Exercises for Self-Reflection   59

Mindfulness Techniques for Healing   61

CHAPTER 7: NAVIGATING DARK MOMENTS   65

Coping Strategies for Setbacks   66

Building Resilience in the Face of Challenges   66

CHAPTER 8: Embracing Light: A Journey to Healing   70

Sustainable Practices for Continued Mental Wellness　71

Fostering Supportive Environments　72

APPENDIX　75

Mental Health Organizations and Helplines　75

About The Author

Veronica L. Vanhoose, the author of this intriguing piece, is a woman who has triumphantly overcome the clutches of depression. Her journey towards healing and self-discovery has shaped her into the resilient and passionate individual she is today. Her battle with depression was not an easy one. It consumed her and cast a shadow over every aspect of her life.

But through sheer determination and unwavering support from her loved ones, she found the strength to rise above her darkest moments. Her journey towards recovery was a long and arduous one; however, it was during this process that she discovered her love for writing as a form of therapy. Now, as a happily married woman and a mother of two beautiful children, Veronica's perspective on life has completely transformed.

She cherishes every moment with her family, knowing firsthand the value of happiness and mental well-being. Through her writing, she aims to inspire and uplift others who may be facing their own battles. Veronica believes that sharing her story can provide solace and hope to those who may feel lost in the depths of their own struggles.

In her writing, Veronica delves into various themes, exploring the complexities of human emotion and the power of resilience. She crafts her words with precision, painting vivid images that resonate with readers on a deeply emotional level. Through her stories, she encourages others to find solace in their own journeys and embrace the beauty that lies within their own unique narratives.

She hopes to touch the hearts of readers and remind them that there is always light at the end of even the darkest tunnels.

My Journey From Darkness To Light

In the depths of my despair, I found myself lost in a never-ending sea of darkness. Depression had consumed me, leaving me feeling hopeless and defeated. But little did I know, this was just the beginning of my journey from darkness to light.

Overcoming depression seemed like an impossible feat. The weight of sadness and emptiness clung to me like a heavy cloak, suffocating any glimpse of joy that dared to enter my life. It was in this state of despair that I realized I needed help. I reached out to a therapist, hoping that they would be the guiding light to lead me out of this darkness.

Therapy became my lifeline, my safe haven in a world that seemed so cold and unforgiving. In those sessions, I confronted my deepest fears and traumas, unraveling the tangled mess that had led me into the abyss of depression. With each passing session, I began to see glimmers of hope. The therapy was not a quick fix, but it provided me with the tools and support I needed to navigate my way towards the light.

Alongside therapy, exercise became an integral part of my journey towards healing. Each morning, I laced up my running shoes and hit the pavement. The rhythmic pounding of my feet against the ground became a metaphor for the strength and resilience I was slowly cultivating within myself. As the miles passed by, I could feel the weight of depression lifting, replaced by a sense of accomplishment and vitality.

But perhaps the most crucial aspect of my journey was the unwavering support of my loved ones. They became my pillars of strength, standing by my side through the darkest nights and celebrating each small victory with me. Their love and encouragement reminded me that I was not alone in this battle. Together, we fought against the shadows, one step at a time.

And so, as I reflect on my journey from darkness to light, I am filled with gratitude for the lessons learned and the strength gained. Overcoming depression was not a linear path, but rather a winding road filled with obstacles and setbacks. However, through therapy, exercise, and the unwavering support of loved ones, I emerged from the depths of darkness into a world filled with light, hope, and possibility.

CHAPTER 1: INTRODUCTION

Welcome to the book "Beneath the Shadows: Illuminating the Path Out of Depression." Within these pages, we will take a deep dive into the world of depression, a complicated and sometimes misunderstood terrain. This book is more than just words on a page; it is a source of knowledge, compassion, and—above all—hope.

I want you to know that you are not alone as you embark on this quest. I express in this introduction my personal connection to the topic as well as my dedication to this important conversation. My goal is to establish a bridge of understanding between the writer and the reader by sharing my own experiences with depression and bringing attention to the problems that are frequently overlooked.

Recognizing that a complex web of emotions, triggers, and cultural beliefs lurks behind the surface of depression is the first step in our journey. The goal of the trip is to both uncover the hidden dimensions of this mental health issue and direct you toward a resilient and healing route.

This book is an offering, a synthesis of useful tools, thoughts, and the experience of others who have walked similar journeys. It is evidence of the capacity for change and the inner power. Let's work together to cast light on the darkness and pave the way for a happier, more optimistic tomorrow.

Purpose of the book

By exposing its hidden facets and busting myths about depression, this book aims to promote a thorough and compassionate knowledge of the condition. To provide useful advice and insights to people negotiating the challenges of depression, shedding light on a route to recovery and wellbeing.

It also offers real-life accounts of those who have overcome depression, inspiring and giving hope to others who are currently struggling with mental health issues. Not to mention enhancing the dialogue about mental health in general, spreading knowledge, and lessening the stigma attached to depression.

It usually provides readers with useful tools, activities, and mindfulness practices that can support them on their individual path to recovery.Finally, promote the creation of supportive settings by highlighting the value of community, compassion, and understanding while dealing with mental health issues.

Overview of Depression and it's Prevalence

Major depressive disorder, or depression, is a prevalent and dangerous medical condition that has an adverse effect on one's emotions, thoughts, and behavior. Thankfully, there is treatment for it. Sadness and/or a loss of interest in once-enjoyed activities are symptoms of depression. It can impair your ability to perform at work and at home and cause a range of mental and physical issues.

A depressive state is not the same as normal mood swings or sentiments related to daily living. It may have an impact on many facets of life, including ties to friends, family, and the community. It may originate from or contribute to issues at work and in the classroom.

Anyone can experience depression. Depression is more likely to strike those who have experienced abuse, significant losses, or other stressful situations. A depressed episode is not the same as normal mood swings. For at least two weeks, they last for the majority of the day, almost every day.For a diagnosis of depression, symptoms must be present for at least two weeks and indicate a decline in your pre-disordered functional level.

It's crucial to rule out general medical reasons because certain medical diseases, such as thyroid issues, brain tumors, or vitamin deficiencies, can mirror the symptoms of depression also. Moreover, a few symptoms are as follows:

- Inadequate focus
- Overwhelming guilt or poor self-worth,
- Hopelessness about the future,
- Suicidal thoughts,
- Disturbed sleep,
- Changes in eating or weight, and
- Extreme exhaustion or low energy.

Women are more likely to have depression than men.

An estimated 3.8% of people suffer from depression, including 5.7% of individuals over 60 and 5% of adults (4% of males and 6% of women).

1. Depression affects over 280 million individuals worldwide. Women are around 50% more likely than males to experience depression.
2. Over 10% of women who are pregnant or recently gave birth experience depression globally.

An estimated 700,000 people lose their lives to suicide each year. The fourth most common cause of mortality for those aged 15 to 29 is suicide.

CHAPTER 2: UNVEILING THE SHADOWS

Unveiling the Shadows: Navigating the Depths of Mental Health" is a compelling exploration into the intricate and often concealed realms of the human psyche. In this journey, individuals are encouraged to confront the shadows—those hidden recesses of their emotions and thoughts that may contribute to the complexities of mental health challenges. The process involves an introspective odyssey, guiding individuals to acknowledge, understand, and ultimately embrace the multifaceted nature of their inner world.

The metaphorical "shadows" represent the uncharted territories of suppressed emotions, unresolved traumas, and unspoken fears. By unveiling these shadows, individuals embark on a courageous endeavor to shed light on aspects of themselves that may have long been obscured. This process is not only about acknowledging the struggles but also about reclaiming agency and self-compassion. It paves the way for a transformative journey toward healing, offering a roadmap for individuals to navigate the intricacies of mental health with resilience and self-awareness.

This is an invitation to challenge the stigma surrounding mental health and foster a compassionate dialogue. It encourages a collective acknowledgment of the shadows within us all, recognizing that vulnerability is not a sign of weakness but a testament to our shared humanity. Through this exploration, individuals find the strength to confront their shadows, fostering a deeper understanding of themselves and creating a foundation for sustained mental well-being.

Understanding the Root Causes

This investigation of the complex network of variables causing depression is very important. This section explores how biological, psychological, and environmental factors interact to reveal the intricacies that frequently underlie this mental health issue.

By traversing the complex terrain and providing readers with insights into the many causes of sadness, authors may address everything from genetic predispositions to the effects of prior experiences. It also acknowledges that a variety of circumstances that are particular to each person frequently combine to cause depression. These many elements, which might serve as depression triggers, include:

Biological Factors

Complex connections between the brain and body are involved in biological variables that predispose individuals to depression. These factors include hormone imbalances, brain chemistry, and heredity. Among them are:

Genetics: Genetic factors can impact a familial propensity to depression, rendering individuals more vulnerable if there is a family history of the disorder.

Neurotransmitter imbalances: Mistakes in neurotransmitters, including norepinephrine, serotonin, and dopamine, can affect how the body regulates mood and exacerbate depressed symptoms.

Hormone Changes: Mood swings and the development of depression can be caused by variations in hormone levels, especially during significant life events such as puberty, pregnancy, and menopause.

Brain Function and Structure: Depression has been associated with abnormalities in the amygdala and hippocampus, among other brain areas.

Inflammation: As the relationship between the immune system and mental health becomes more clear, chronic inflammation in the body may contribute to depression.

Psychological Triggers

Aspects of cognition, emotions, and personal coping strategies are all involved in psychological variables that contribute to depression, such as unresolved conflicts, traumatic experiences in the past, and negative thinking patterns. Here are a few crucial psychological elements:

Trauma and Stressful Life Events: Significant life stresses or past traumas can have a negative impact on an individual's ability to detect and deal with future problems, which can lead to the development of depression.

Cognitive Patterns: Persistent self-criticism, pessimism, or skewed thinking are examples of negative thought patterns that might increase one's susceptibility to depression.

Personality tendencies: Having certain tendencies, including perfectionism, poor self-esteem, or an inclination to absorb bad events, might make depression more likely to occur.

Coping Strategies: The continuation of depressed symptoms might be attributed to ineffective coping techniques, such as harmful habits or avoidance.

Interpersonal Relationships: A depressive state can be exacerbated by interpersonal difficulties, social isolation, or a lack of a supporting social network.

Environmental Influences

The following external elements, which have an impact on the development and aggravation of depression, are examples of how the environment can have an impact:

Stressful Life Events: Significant life transitions, such the death of a loved one, financial hardships, or job loss, can hasten the onset of depression.

Family Dynamics: Support networks, relationships, and family dynamics all have a big impact on mental health. Depression may be exacerbated by dysfunctional family dynamics or a dearth of helpful social networks.

Social Isolation: Depression symptoms may be exacerbated by a lack of social ties, loneliness, or social isolation. Having a strong social support system is frequently essential for mental health.

Socioeconomic Factors: Stressors that raise the risk of depression might include financial difficulties, poverty, or limited access to resources and education.

Cultural and Societal Expectations: Discrimination, cultural expectations, and societal pressures may all lead to despondency or feelings of inadequacy, which can have an adverse effect on one's mental health.

Neurobiological Considerations

Examining the complex relationships between the structure and function of the brain and their bearing on mental health is one of the main goals of neurobiological considerations in the context of depression. Important elements consist of:

Amygdala and Hippocampus: Depression is connected to alterations in the amygdala's (which processes emotions) and hippocampus's (which is linked to memory and emotions) size and activity.

Neuroplasticity: The brain's capacity for self-organization and adaptation is a critical factor to take into account. Neuroplasticity—the brain's capacity to adjust to new experiences—may be impacted by depression.

Neurotransmitter Function: Communication between brain cells can be impacted by disruptions in neurotransmitter systems, including those involving serotonin, dopamine, and norepinephrine. This can lead to depression symptoms.

Endocrine System: The hypothalamus-pituitary-adrenal (HPA) axis is one of the endocrine system's interactions with the brain that regulates stress responses. This system can become dysregulated in depression.

Exploring Hidden Emotions and Triggers

Identify Suppressed feelings: Gain insight into feelings that you may have repressed or ignored, enabling a more candid assessment of your inner landscape.

Identify Triggers: Examine the particular circumstances, incidents, or ideas that set off depressive episodes in order to raise awareness of the patterns that lead to emotional downturns.

Validate Feelings: Stress that a critical first step toward emotional well-being is to recognize and validate all feelings, including those that are difficult or painful.

Promote Self-Reflection: Promote self-reflection to help people understand the emotional intricacies that could be involved in their experiences with depression.

Impact of Stigmas and Misconceptions

Telling someone you are depressed entails a risk of arousing emotions in others that might vary from perplexity to suspicion and contempt. For many persons with depression, feelings of personal stigma are so ubiquitous that they are an intrinsic part of the condition. Many people just do not see depression as a medical condition, and they find it difficult to comprehend why certain people are unable to "pull themselves together" or "snap out of it."

In my opinion, this makes about as much sense as advising someone who has diabetes to wake up from a coma or an epileptic to stop having fits which is not proper behavior, yet a lot of others who are close to depressed individuals tell them just that. Feelings of humiliation, shame, and self-disgust are common among sufferers due to centuries of misinterpreting the condition and a societal and political viewpoint that has resisted the growth of empathy for those with mood disorders.

Because they continue to believe certain myths about depression, many people choose not to get treatment. Among these are:

Depression is rare and will not happen to me

Anybody can experience depression, regardless of their age, ethnicity, or sex. It is one of the most prevalent mental health issues, impacting 121 million individuals globally1. According to estimates from the World Health Organization, 5–10% of individuals may require depression treatment at any point in their lives, and 8–20% of people are at risk of developing depression at some point in their lives.

Depression is about feeling sad

Suffering is only one aspect of depression. One of the signs of depression is having persistently low moods. Depression, however, can also include behavioral changes like losing interest in daily activities, mental symptoms like feelings of worthlessness, and physical symptoms like changes in food and sleep quality. When a person is depressed, these symptoms last longer than two weeks.

Depression is a sign of weakness

Depression is a medical illness, not a sign of weakness. Treatment options exist for the chemical imbalance that causes depression.

Like diabetes or asthma, depression is a terrible medical illness that has nothing to do with a person's character. Major life events that might be difficult to handle, such losing a career or a loved one, can frequently set off depression.

Depression is temporary and will go away by itself

Depression is not going to go away on its own. It's a medical problem that has to be supported and treated. In fact, if depression treatment is not received, symptoms are likely to worsen. Therefore, it's critical to undergo treatment as soon as possible to stop the worsening of depression symptoms.

Depression is incurable.

Of all the mental health illnesses, depression is one of the easiest to treat. According to data from the World Health Organization, between 60 and 80 percent of people react favorably to a combination of medicine and psychotherapy therapies.3. Everyone's recuperation period is different. You may enjoy a normal and productive life if you receive therapy early. However, it's critical to realize that depression therapy is a lengthy process, and recovery might take many months.

Depression can only be treated by medication

Medication is just one kind of depression therapy that is accessible. Additional treatments for depression include lifestyle modifications, counseling, and psychiatric intervention. Each patient may have unique therapeutic needs. For some people, medicine may be the most useful treatment; for others, psychological assistance may be the most beneficial; yet others may benefit most from a mix of therapies. In order to create a personalized support plan and learn more about various treatment options, it is therefore important to speak with a mental health specialist.

I'm hesitant to discuss my depression for fear that doing so may make it worsen.

You may express your emotions, look for validation, and come up with answers when you talk about your feelings. It might be beneficial for you to speak with a qualified counselor who can assist you in overcoming depression. All provided information is treated with utmost confidentiality.

People believe that I am lazy rather than sad, thus they don't think I need a doctor.

A person suffering from depression loses a lot of energy. It's normal to lose interest in routine activities, therefore it shouldn't be seen as a sign of laziness.

It's all in your head.

A few people contest that depression is an actual medical condition. In actuality, depression is a real medical illness with roots in the chemistry, structure, and function of the brain, as well as occasionally involving biological or environmental variables. Extreme fatigue, excessive sleepiness, and aches and pains are some of the signs of depression. People may also experience dejection, uncertainty about themselves, and pessimism as a result of it. Suicidal ideation is not unusual. It's critical to understand that depression is curable with medicine and/or psychotherapy, and that healing is achievable.

Depression only affects women

Men aren't often encouraged in our culture to talk about their emotions, seek for assistance, or display vulnerability. Consequently, some guys decide not to receive therapy. The American Foundation for Suicide Prevention states that men are four times more likely than women to die by suicide, with white males over 45 being the most susceptible. You are not alone if you are a male going through despair or thinking about ending your life. The National Institute of Mental Health reports that almost six million American males experience depression annually. Men also need to receive mental health therapy, and this is something that our culture needs to recognize.

Depression is a sign of weakness

Anybody, regardless of physical or mental power, can be affected by depression. Judy Collins, Terry Bradshaw, and Abraham Lincoln are among the most well-known Americans who have battled depression. One of the greatest boxers of all time, Oscar De La Hoya, has received treatment for depression. He holds ten world titles in six different weight classes.

Discussing it only makes things worse.

If you see depressive symptoms in your partner, kids, or coworkers, try not to dismiss them. Offering assistance may be quite beneficial to the one experiencing depression. When someone detects a shift in your behavior or attitude and has the guts and compassion to inquire about how you're doing, it is a relief. Family and friends may be a great support system for someone going through depression by listening and offering steady support and encouragement.

Medication will change your personality and you'll be taking it forever

Antidepressants of today are both efficient and safe. Antidepressant medication helps most individuals feel more like themselves. Antidepressants don't usually make individuals feel "medicated," nor do they have the same effects as sedatives or painkillers. Their task is to rectify the chemical imbalance in your brain that is resulting in depressive symptoms. When you feel healthy enough to cease taking a medicine, your doctor will assist you in determining if it is helping you. Generally speaking, taking an antidepressant and attending therapy will expedite your recuperation.

The best way to help someone with depression is to cheer them up

Those with good intentions will frequently advise someone who is depressed to see the bright side of things. or get over it. or give it up. But it's far more intricate than that. Ensuring that a person with depression has access to screening and therapy is the greatest approach to support them. A depression screening can be conducted in-person during your primary care visit, over the phone in private with a discreet call to a crisis hotline, or at an intake session at a counseling center.

CHAPTER 3: ILLUMINATING SIGHTS

ThiThis page encourages individuals navigating depression to find glimpses of brightness even in the darkest corners. It also invites a deliberate shift in perception, urging those grappling with depression to seek out the subtle hues of hope and resilience within their own experiences. The concept of "illuminating sights" becomes a powerful metaphor, prompting a conscious effort to uncover moments of beauty, even when obscured by the shadows of despair.

By consciously seeking out these illuminating sights, individuals navigating depression can find small yet profound sources of solace and inspiration, paving the way for a path toward healing and rediscovery of the radiance within their own lives.

Unveiling Emotional Depths

Types of Depression

There are many different types of depression. Understanding the different types of depression is crucial for proper diagnosis and treatment.

Major Depressive Disorder

Most of the time, people with severe depressive illness, sometimes referred to as clinical depression, will have extremely depressing sensations. Major depressive disorder Signs of depression that are more prevalent include:

- Unexpected weight increase or reduction.
- A decrease in enthusiasm or enjoyment for once-enjoyable activities.
- Difficulties sleeping.
- Sensations of exhaustion and low energy.
- Sentiments of shame, worthlessness, or hopelessness.
- Difficulties staying focused or making decisions.
- Feeling the want to hurt oneself.

It's critical to recognize that many persons experience severe depressive disorder in different ways. Not all people have the same symptoms.

Persistent Depressive Disorder

A prolonged kind of depression that lasts for two years or more is called persistent depressive disorder. The following are some of the most typical signs of chronic depressive disorder:

- Issues related to appetite (eating excessively or not at all).
- Needing to sleep either too little or more than normal.
- Weariness or a lack of vitality.
- Difficulties including poor self-esteem.
- Difficulties paying attention and concentrating.
- Difficulties with depressing, empty, and gloomy feelings.

People with persistent depressive illness may find it difficult to manage their symptoms over the long term, even when they are not as severe as those of a major depressive episode.

Seasonal Affective Disorder

A person may experience symptoms of seasonal affective disorder (SAD) during one time of year, usually in the winter. People go through the following depressive symptoms at this time:

- Sadness
- Energy deficiency Loss of enthusiasm for activities
- inability to concentrate.
- Hopelessness
- Sleeping for extended periods of time
- Difficulties with thoughts of self-harm

Typically, spring and summer are when seasonal affective disorder disappears. However, a mental health expert may suggest a more comprehensive treatment plan based on the severity of the depression.

Postpartum Depression

A few days or after giving birth, postpartum depression sets in. Postpartum depression symptoms include:

- Sadness
- Bonding with your infant is difficult,
- Crying a lot
- Fear that I'm not a good mother
- Panic episodes and anxiety
- Feelings of hopelessness, including thoughts of hurting oneself or your child

This kind of sadness, known as peripartum depression, can strike some women at any point throughout their pregnancy.

It's critical to realize that postpartum depression is not an indication of weakness, imperfection, or failure of any kind. Given the complexity of pregnancy and childbirth, women who are suffering from postpartum depression need a great deal of understanding and assistance at this time.

High Functioning Depression

Despite having depressive symptoms, people with high-functioning depression are able to operate in a variety of spheres of life, such as relationships, employment, and education. When someone has high-functioning depression, their symptoms may be less severe, or they may discover coping mechanisms or ways to completely hide their depressive symptoms.

Depression Signs and Symptoms

Depression is a difficult mental health issue. The severity of a person's symptoms might vary depending on whether they are classified as mild, moderate, or severe depression.

Among the most typical signs of depression are:

Psychological symptoms:

- Challenges with a lack of motivation or interest in usual activities
- Challenges with low self-esteem
- Experiencing feelings of guilt
- Challenges with decision-making
- Challenges with feelings of anxiety, stress, or worry
- Consistent challenges with sadness or low mood
- Consistent challenges with feelings of hopelessness and helpless
- Challenges with low self-esteem

- Experiencing feelings of guilt
- Feeling irritable and intolerant of others
- Mood swings
- Experiencing self-harming thoughts

Physical symptoms:

- Speaking and moving more slowly than usual
- Experiencing changes in appetite or weight
- Unexplained pain
- Experiencing a lack of energy
- Loss of libido
- Changes in the menstrual cycle
- Challenges with sleep patterns

Social symptoms:

- Sudden social withdrawal
- Avoiding hobbies or once-beloved activities
- Challenges with relationships at home, work or friends

Symptoms of Depression in Children

It's important to remember that a child does not always have depression just because they seem unhappy or disturbed.

Consult a mental health professional for guidance if depressive symptoms worsen and start to interfere with regular activities like friendships, family, or schooling.

Among the most typical signs of depression in kids are:

- difficulties sleeping longer than normal
- difficulties concentrating and maintaining attention
- Social disengagement from loved ones
- difficulties with self-worth and confidence
- symptoms of an appetite loss or eating more than normal
- Having trouble relaxing
- Having shame or worthlessness sentiments
- Feeling empty
- Problems with suicidal ideation
- Signs of self-destructive conduct

Recognizing the Need for Change

Like many other issues in life, there are some things we can affect over time, other things we have more immediate power over, and some things we have no control over at all. Before taking any action to bring about change, we should consider if the things we wish to see happen are truly within our control.

For instance, we may discover that certain individuals in our lives are a cause of stress. We might attempt to discuss potential adjustments with them, but unless they acknowledge the problem and are prepared to take action, the problem will mostly stay uncontrollable.

We can spend a lot of time and effort trying to alter things, but when we stop to think about it, we find that we really don't have much power to do it. The lesson here is not to give up on the hard things; rather, it is to direct our energy toward the areas where it will truly make a difference, instead of squandering it on ineffective endeavors, and to establish reasonable, attainable objectives in accordance with those areas.

We are unlikely to accomplish all of our goals at once, especially if we are experiencing worry and sadness, which makes every step feel more difficult.

After suffering from depression for a long time, some people essentially change. Eliminating their despair would entail taking away a portion of their (perceived) identity. Without it, they would have to face life, which is difficult when you don't even know who you are. It's up to you to reconstruct yourself and save what you can, which is an arduous and scary endeavor that exposes you.

An other factor related to vulnerability is the anxieties that accompany enjoyment. The crash, or raising your expectations just to have them dashed again, is a concern that many who are depressed harbor. It aches more and more with each fall. Simply said, staying down is safer and easier.

You cannot heal depression until you acknowledge that change is necessary, which is the first stage in treating depression, then focus all of your attention on improving and becoming joyful.

Every depressed patient has a different requirement for adjustments, and you should seek quick assistance when you;

- Consider harming oneself or other people, or have suicidal thoughts and desires
- lack the stamina or motivation to carry out your responsibilities, such as caring for your children.
- believe your symptoms are getting worse.

CHAPTER 4: REDISCOVERING JOY

In the depths of depression, the pursuit of joy may seem like an elusive endeavor, obscured by the shadows that cast a pall over every aspect of life. However, the journey of "Rediscovering Joy" is a testament to the resilience of the human spirit and the capacity for transformation. It begins with a profound shift in perspective, an intentional turning toward the present moment with mindful awareness. This shift lays the foundation for the rediscovery of joy in the seemingly mundane aspects of life.

One avenue toward joy involves engaging in positive activities that resonate with individual passions and interests. By incorporating these activities into daily life, individuals can create spaces for moments of genuine happiness and accomplishment. Whether it's a creative pursuit, a physical activity, or a simple act of kindness, these endeavors become beacons of light in the journey toward emotional well-being.

Connection and support form another vital pillar in the process of rediscovering joy. Meaningful connections with others, whether friends, family, or support groups, provide a shared space where joy can be nurtured. Sharing experiences, both the challenges and triumphs, fosters a sense of belonging and solidarity, creating a supportive network that acknowledges the importance of joy in the healing process.

Below are the various evidence-based strategies and interventions designed to support individuals on their journey out of depression.

1. Therapy

- Interpersonal therapy (IPT)
- Cognitive-behavioral therapy (CBT)
- Acceptance and commitment therapy (ACT)
- Mindfulness-based cognitive therapy (MBCT)

2. Medication and Psychopharmacology

3. Brain stimulation therapy

- Electroconvulsive Therapy
- Repetitive Transcranial Magnetic Stimulation
- Vagus Nerve Stimulation

Therapeutic Approaches

Interpersonal Therapy (IPT)

A traumatic event or depressive symptoms can occasionally have an impact on many areas of your life, including your relationships.

Sometimes, though, it might go the other way around, with your relationship problems causing you to feel depressed.

Interpersonal psychotherapy's (IPT) primary goal is to assist you in resolving these interpersonal issues and difficulties in order to enhance your emotional state.

What is IPT therapy?

A focused, brief therapeutic method, interpersonal psychotherapy, also known as interpersonal therapy, typically lasts 12 to 16 weeks. Weekly scheduling and a 50-minute duration are usual for sessions. It is intended to assist you in controlling severe mood disorders and enhancing social interactions.

This kind of therapy is predicated on a depressive medical paradigm. This implies that interpersonal difficulties are seen as triggers for clinical depression and clinical depression itself as a biological tendency.

IPT emphasizes that you are never "at fault" for depression or other mood disorders. Rather, it is thought that you may be predisposed to certain symptoms either biologically or by inheritance. Interpersonal conflict and other stressful life events might trigger them.

But even while there may be biological components to depression, if you concentrate on treating the interpersonal issues that triggered this underlying biological condition, you may control your symptoms.

Clinical research has demonstrated that symptoms of depression and other mood disorders are likely to go away if you can successfully handle an interpersonal issue. This is IPT's primary goal.

What ages is IPT for?

Both individual and group treatment are possible forms of interpersonal psychotherapy. From teenagers to elderly folks, it has undergone extensive adaptation to suit their needs.

IPT has been modified to become IPT-A (interpersonal psychotherapy-adolescents) for teenagers between the ages of 12 and 18. IPT-A likewise lasts around 12 to 16 sessions, just like the adult version does. It focuses on the connections between difficulties in relationships and the development or persistence of depressive and other mental health symptoms.

A paradigm known as FB-IPT (family-based interpersonal psychotherapy) was developed to incorporate more parental engagement in IPT-A for children under the age of twelve. Early research indicates that treating youngsters between the ages of 7 and 12 may be beneficial.

Stages of IPT

IPT is based on a structured plan and develops in three phases:

1. Beginning

It focuses on determining the interpersonal issue area that needs attention and lasts one to three sessions.

You can be asked to enumerate all of your key relationships, both past and present, along with your feelings about each one. In addition, your therapist might want to go over your prior therapy sessions and personal medical history.

They will decide how to proceed with the remainder of the therapy based on all of this.

2. Middle

Your therapist will now concentrate on treating the difficulty area, which might be mourning, role shift, role conflict, or interpersonal inadequacies, based on what they discovered and developed during the first phase.

Establishing and treating the connection between your mood symptoms and this problematic region will also be a focus of this phase.

Typically, the middle phase lasts from session 4 to session 14.

In these sessions, you and your therapist may discuss several approaches to addressing interpersonal difficulties. Another option is to concentrate on discovering novel, adaptable habits for handling situations in the future.

Decision analysis and communication will also be the main topics of these intermediate courses.

Your therapist will urge you to put your newly discovered answers to use in the real world, even if you won't be sending homework home.

In your upcoming sessions, you may go over these new experiences and talk about how these techniques worked.

Your therapist would advise you to practice the new tactic in future situations if it worked well. You might come up with fresh ideas for dealing with these issues if you didn't think it went well or you weren't comfortable.

3. End

The last two or three meetings will be devoted to assessing your development. Focusing on role transitions in relation to therapy's finish may also be part of it.

Most likely, you'll talk about your previous sessions and your feelings on the treatment plan. Together with your therapist, you may decide to focus on additional topics in the future.

Your therapist may suggest further sessions to address maintenance concerns and relapse prevention if your symptoms persist.

IPT Techniques

During the first few sessions, your therapist will focus on reviewing the status and quality of your most significant relationships. This includes:

- determining the sources of your social support
- attachment styles
- communication styles
- specific interpersonal challenges you may be facing at the moment or in the past.

The therapist will suggest one area of concentration for the remaining sessions based on this evaluation.

IPT focuses on four primary areas of interpersonal difficulty that might exacerbate depressive symptoms. Therapy often focuses on one of these areas:

If the loss of a loved one is the cause of your symptoms, you may be experiencing grief or complex mourning.

If you are finding it difficult to adjust to changes in social roles, role shifting may be the best option for you. For instance, changing careers, relationships, or transitioning from being a student to an employee.

If your symptoms are linked to problems in a relationship where roles are not reciprocal or satisfying, then interpersonal role disputes are the main emphasis.

Deficiencies in interpersonal relationships are the focus if the onset of your symptoms is not linked to a specific event, but instead you have experienced long standing challenges in interpersonal relationships

Primary goal of IPT

Improving your symptoms and interpersonal interactions is the primary objective of IPT. The theory is that these symptoms of mood will ultimately go away if you address the interpersonal issues that are related to your current state of being.

Your social support system and relationships will get stronger as you recover. This will thus help to alleviate your symptoms and stop any relapses.

Cognitive-behavioral Therapy (CBT)

Cognitive behavioral therapy (CBT) is a popular, evidence-based psychotherapy that has benefited a large number of patients worldwide.

By reevaluating faulty thinking processes, cognitive behavioral therapy (CBT) aims to assist you in adapting and changing your mentality and actions.

If you're seeking for evidence-based treatment to reduce chronic mental health problems, CBT may be a useful tool, regardless of whether you're concerned about little things or have a mental health illness.

How does cognitive behavioral therapy work?

In essence, CBT involves recognizing, addressing, and altering harmful thought patterns so that, with practice, your outlook, actions, and general well-being all improve.

It should be simpler to modify your conduct in the future, for example, if you alter your feelings about particular circumstances.

Adverse thinking may manifest in various ways in mental health disorders such as depression, anxiety, substance abuse, phobias, and many more. Examples of these include:

Thinking in binary terms, making excessive generalizations, concentrating on the bad, and catastrophizing.

Together with your therapist, you will utilize CBT to pinpoint the thought patterns that are upsetting you. This is a crucial step in controlling excessive feelings and destructive habits.

Contrary to popular belief, which holds that treatment consists solely of talking with a therapist, CBT is highly organized and individualized. You'll eventually pick up CBT skills to identify and disprove negative beliefs.

What can I expect from CBT?

Your therapist will likely ask you to complete a questionnaire before treatment even starts. This questionnaire will be used to evaluate your mental health and monitor your progress over time.

In order to tailor the course of therapy for you, they will probably spend the most of the first session getting to know you and your mental processes through questioning.

Since cognitive behavioral therapy (CBT) is a team effort, it's critical that you and your therapist click. Don't get discouraged, even if it might be time-consuming and frustrating, don't be afraid to meet with multiple therapists until you find one that you're happy with.

After completing all the fundamental questions, deciding on your objectives, and identifying any erroneous thought patterns, your therapist may collaborate with you to select the most appropriate methods for evaluating and correcting those ideas.

Expect to receive assignments as well. Outside of sessions, CBT frequently incorporates readings, behavioral exercises, and self-reflection assignments.

Even while CBT is often conducted in person, there are efficient online alternatives as well.

CBT strategies

- Recording your ideas and going over them again at a later time.
- Tackling anxious circumstances in order to acquire coping skills.
- Working on problem-solving techniques with your counselor.
- Interacting with others through role-playing.

You can acquire beneficial abilities like the following by using CBT techniques like these at home alone and with your therapist:

- Becoming conscious of harmful ideas and how they affect your feelings.
- Gaining a better rational comprehension of the behavior of others.
- Putting automated assumptions to the test.
- Evaluating reality with precision.
- Managing stressful or provoking circumstances.
- Acquiring skills for relaxation and confidence building through positive self-talk.

Applying the abilities you acquire in treatment to your everyday life is the goal. It is similar to strengthening any muscle by training it, except in this case, the muscle is your brain.

It calls for cooperation, dedication, and open communication between you and your therapist.

What are the benefits of CBT?

It frequently produces long-term effects: The benefits of CBT can continue long after therapy is finished since the focus is on recognizing maladaptive thought patterns and developing practical skills.

It's a useful substitute for medication because some individuals find that it doesn't work for them. CBT provides an alternative therapy method that takes a totally different approach.

The course of therapy is somewhat brief: CBT doesn't need to last for years, in contrast to other forms of talk therapy. It can take five to twenty sessions, with the possibility of a few follow-up sessions being helpful.

CBT can be conducted in groups, one-on-one, or even alone: The format of the CBT technique is variable even though treatment is regimented.

The skills you'll learn can help beyond your original reason for treatment: The abilities that CBT frequently promotes, such as time management, interpersonal communication, and problem-solving, can benefit you in a variety of spheres of your life..

Acceptance and Commitment Therapy (ACT)

Acceptance and commitment therapy (ACT) is an intervention that uses numerous behavior-changing techniques and mindfulness to enhance psychological flexibility.

The tenet of ACT is that our problems are not limited to the traumatic events in our life. Instead, a large portion of our suffering stems from our attempts to suppress the unpleasant emotions and memories associated with these encounters.

With the help of Acceptance and Commitment Therapy (ACT), you may learn to stop resisting and over-analyzing your ideas, feelings, and experiences.

Although stress and tough emotions are a natural part of being human, ACT helps you identify and address the underlying causes of these feelings.

ACT is based on six core values:

- **Acceptance:** Accepting your thoughts and feelings.
- Cognitive diffusion: Recognizing your thoughts as just thoughts, not facts.
- **Present moment awareness**: Focusing on what is happening within you and your environment.
- **Self-as context**: Recognizing that you are not your thoughts and feelings. Simply observe them.
- **Values:** Pinpointing your priorities in life and recognizing what motivates you and gives you meaning.
- **Committed action**: Taking action on your values to create a fulfilling life.

ACT might be prolonged over a longer time period or it can be short term.

At last, you pick up behaviors that might lead to a more fulfilling existence.

Mindfulness-based Cognitive Therapy (MBCT)

Group psychotherapy known as mindfulness-based cognitive therapy, or MBCT, blends cognitive behavioral therapy (CBT) with mindfulness practices like yoga and meditation.

These are the kinds of tactics taught in MBCT to stop automatic thoughts and sensations that might lead to depression. Additionally, clients learn how to distinguish themselves from their ideas and feelings, which may lessen depressive symptoms.

The original purpose of MBCT was to keep those who had previously experienced depression from relapsing. Still, it can benefit those suffering from a variety of mental illnesses.

All things considered, MBCT is an 8-week organized group program that meets once a week for two to three hours. Every day, clients are given homework tasks that include mindfulness meditation and audio recordings to listen to.

Medication and Psychopharmacology

The term "psychopharmacology" describes the use of drugs to address mental health issues. Most mental health issues can be improved with the use of medications. While some people receive treatment only through medicine, others also receive therapy or other forms of treatment.

Most mental health issues may be effectively treated with a mix of medication and psychotherapy, according to study. A number of drugs may be needed to treat certain illnesses. When several psychiatric drugs are recommended or when medication has to be monitored, a psychiatrist should be consulted.

How do I know if I need medication for a mental health condition?

When symptoms are mild to severe or treatment alone has not made them better, medication is frequently advised. Occasionally, a therapist may, in the interest of their professional judgment, suggest a meeting with a psychiatrist. A psychiatrist can provide an assessment and talk about the potential role drugs might play in therapy for anybody who is interested in finding out if taking medication could be beneficial. Only licensed medical professionals, such as psychiatrists or nurse practitioners, are authorized to administer psychiatric drugs.

How long will I take psychiatric medications?

Psychiatric drugs may be utilized in some cases to temporarily relieve symptoms. In some situations, drugs could work better over an extended length of time. Depending on what the patient and the psychiatrist think is the best course of action for treating a mental health illness, the length of time a patient uses medication might vary from a few weeks or months to several years. It is preferable to work with a treating psychiatrist when making decisions about beginning or quitting medication. Together, the patient and the healthcare professional assess the advantages of drugs against any potential dangers or side effects.

Common classes of medications include:

Antidepressants:

- SSRIs (Selective Serotonin Reuptake Inhibitors): e.g., fluoxetine, sertraline.
- SNRIs (Serotonin-Norepinephrine Reuptake Inhibitors): e.g., venlafaxine, duloxetine.
- Tricyclic Antidepressants: e.g., amitriptyline, nortriptyline.
- MAOIs (Monoamine Oxidase Inhibitors): e.g., phenelzine, tranylcypromine.

Anxiolytics:

- Benzodiazepines: e.g., diazepam, lorazepam (often used for short-term anxiety relief).
- Buspirone: An alternative anxiolytic with a different mechanism of action.

Mood Stabilizers:

- Lithium: Primarily used for bipolar disorder to stabilize mood.

- Anticonvulsants: e.g., lamotrigine, valproate, used for mood stabilization.

Antipsychotics:

- Used to manage psychotic symptoms and sometimes as adjuncts in mood disorders.
- Atypical antipsychotics: e.g., quetiapine, olanzapine.

Stimulants:

- Used in the treatment of attention-deficit/hyperactivity disorder (ADHD).
- Examples include methylphenidate and amphetamine derivatives.

Brain Stimulation Therapy

Psychotherapy or pharmaceuticals may not always be effective in treating major depressive disorder (MDD). Your symptoms could subside temporarily before returning, or they might remain unchanged. It's known as depression that is resistant to therapy.

The good news is that brain stimulation treatment is an additional alternative. It stimulates brain activity with the use of magnets, implants, or electricity. The majority of brain stimulation treatments are novel or undergoing research. However, scientists believe they might be useful resources for those with depression who are resistant to therapy. Let's examine the first three.

Electroconvulsive Therapy

The use of electroconvulsive treatment (ECT) dates back more than eight decades. It's the kind of brain stimulation therapy that has been studied the most. It is usually used for bipolar illness or severe depression that is not responding to therapy. According to studies, ECT is effective and safe.

How It Works

Because you will be sleeping during the process, you won't feel anything. You will also be prescribed a muscle relaxant by the doctor to aid in immobility. They will apply adhesive patches to your head that have wires attached to them. We refer to these as electrodes. Controlled electrical pulses cause a seizure that lasts less than a minute after you fall asleep. This has an impact on brain chemicals and neurons. You won't recall what occurred or how it felt when you wake up in a few minutes. After the anesthetic wears off, you can return home and resume your day.

For a total of six to twelve sessions, ECT is normally administered two or three times each week. The number of sessions required will depend on the severity of your symptoms and how quickly you respond.

Side Effects

The most common side effects are:

- Headache
- Nausea
- Fatigue
- Confusion
- Memory loss that lasts from minutes to hours
- Problems learning and short-term memory loss are the biggest risks.

Shorter pulse durations and simply applying electrodes to one side of the head are two solutions that researchers are currently investigating.

Repetitive Transcranial Magnetic Stimulation

Repeated magnetic pulses are used in repetitive transcranial magnetic stimulation (rTMS), which stimulates your brain. Researchers are unsure of how it alleviates sadness. It's possible that it increases nerve cell activity in mood-regulating regions of the brain.

How It Works

It's not necessary to be sleeping to get rTMS. Earplugs are necessary, though. This is because each time the machine pulses, a loud clicking noise is produced. An electromagnetic coil will be applied to the front of your skull by the doctor. Your brain generates electric currents from brief electromagnetic pulses. There will be a "tapping" sensation when the pulses are detected. Since you haven't slept, you can drive yourself home right now.

The optimal number and duration of treatments are yet unknown to scientists. However, meetings last 30 to 40 minutes apiece on average. And they are typically completed for about a month, five days a week.

Side Effects
Common side effects include:

- Headache
- Tingling, twitching, or spasms in your facial muscles
- Feeling lightheaded

These side effects usually go away after your session and may lessen as you continue treatment.

Rare but more serious side effects include:

- Seizures
- Hearing loss, especially if you didn't have enough ear protection during the procedure
- Mania, especially if you have bipolar disorder

Vagus Nerve Stimulation

There is a vagus nerve on each side of your body that runs from your abdomen to your brain. The original purpose of vagus nerve stimulation (VNS) was to cure epilepsy. Yet in certain situations of depression that is resistant to therapy, it also benefits.

How It Works

Your surgeon will insert a tiny battery-operated gadget beneath your skin on the chest during the procedure. Usually, they position it to the left. We refer to this as a pulse generator. The vagus nerve is then connected to an electrical cable that is inserted into your neck by them.

The pulse generator will be activated by your doctor when your operation is healed. It will be programmed to pulse periodically. 30 seconds of nerve stimulation every 5 minutes is a cycle that is often employed.

Surgery risks include:

- Pain where the device was implanted

- Infection
- Difficulty swallowing
- Temporary paralysis of the vocal cords, though this can be permanent
- Bleeding
- Complications from anesthesia
- The device may not work the right way. Or it may move, which you'll need another surgery to fix.

Side Effects

Side effects can include:

- Changes in voice and hoarseness
- Cough
- Shortness of breath
- Difficulty swallowing
- Neck or throat pain
- Burning, prickling, or tingling in the skin
- Vomiting
- Upset stomach
- Headache
- Hypomania or mania

They may get better after a while. If they don't, your doctor can change the pulse strength to see if it helps.

Effectiveness

Everybody reacts in a unique way. Therefore, it is impossible to predict which brain stimulation treatment will be most effective for you, if any at all. It can take many months to observe any changes. To treat their depression, the majority of people still require psychotherapy, antidepressants, or both. Periodic care may be required every week or every few months. Which therapy you get and your symptoms will determine this. Your physician and you can determine what's best.

Practical Steps for Daily Well-being

Set an alarm

It's general information that sleep deprivation is connected to an increase in depression and other mental health issues. But a 2021 research discovered that having an inconsistent sleep pattern might also increase a person's risk of depression – to the same level as not getting enough sleep.

The quality of the sleep we get varies with our sleep habits. And getting regular, high-quality sleep is essential to preserving mental well-being.

For these reasons, even on the weekends when you might not feel the urge to start your day right away, it's a good idea to incorporate waking up and going to bed at the same time into your daily depressive pattern. Setting alarms (both for the day and the night) and commit to a pattern your body and mind can best rely on.

Feed your body healthy foods

Numerous studies indicate a connection between mental health and nutrition. Research indicates that eating a lot of fast food and processed foods may raise your risk of depression, in addition to the well-established link between obesity and sadness.

Moderation is the key to everything. However, if you incorporate eating complete, fresh meals into your daily routine, you could eventually experience improved physical and emotional well-being.

As part of your morning routine for depression, you might want to start by including some fresh fruit in your breakfast, some lean protein in your lunch, and some fresh veggies in your supper.

Research also suggests that decreased blood levels of zinc, copper, manganese, and vitamin D might occur in depressed individuals. Therefore, taking a supplement or consuming meals high in these nutrients may help reduce the symptoms of depression. It has also been demonstrated that magnesium helps those who suffer from mild to major depression.

To find out the right dose and any possible hazards, it's essential to see a healthcare provider before attempting any supplements for depression. Certain supplements may conflict with drugs you may be taking or be hazardous if taken in excess. Before recommending a supplement, your doctor might also want to take a blood test to check for vitamin deficiencies.

Get moving

It might be rather difficult to get oneself to get up and move when you're experiencing depression. But for precisely this reason, including exercise into your regular routine might be beneficial in treating depression.

Exercise and yoga have been linked to a reduction in depressive symptoms, according to research. Furthermore, certain research has even discovered brain pathways that might account for this reaction.

Additionally, you don't need to prepare for a marathon or spend hours at the gym in order to reap the rewards of regular exercise.

Research points to the potential benefits of conducting low- or moderate-intensity exercise, such as walking, for one hour each day, or higher-intensity exercise, such as running, for fifteen minutes each day. And it doesn't have to be an hour in one go. You can break up exercise sessions into shorter time chunks if that works better for you.

You only want to try your best to exercise your body and raise your heart rate every day. A quick stroll with a friend or even just playing outside with your kids or gardening can work the magic.

Remain hydrated

Getting adequate water throughout the day is probably one of the easiest things you can do to keep your mental health in check. Yes, studies have shown that maintaining proper hydration lowers the likelihood of developing depression.

By always having a reusable water bottle with you, you may position yourself for success. If you usually struggle to remember to drink during the day, you might also try setting alarms on your phone.

Consider journaling

Everybody needs a way to express their strong emotions, and writing may provide that. Some study has indicated that expressive writing, or just expressing your ideas and feelings on paper, can be beneficial for those with major depressive illness, albeit not all studies support this finding.

One daily task that you may complete whenever, whenever, and whatever you like is this one. Writing in your diary may be done in any way. All you need to do is make it a habit to write for a few minutes every day, about whatever you choose.

Additionally, if you struggle to start, consider using one of these writing prompts to get your creative juices flowing:

- Which three things would you wish to share with a partner, family member, or friend?

- Which troubling ideas or feelings come to mind most often?
- Which three everyday activities make you the happiest?

Practice mindfulness and meditation.

It might be challenging to slow down and concentrate on the here and now in the hectic world of today. However, evidence indicates that taking precisely that action helps lessen the effects of depression. For some whose depression is resistant to therapy, it could even be helpful.

Finding a peaceful space where you can block out all outside noise for a few minutes every day and just breathe is the basic objective of mindfulness and meditation, however everyone's experience with these practices may vary slightly.

The first step in incorporating meditation into your regular routine is to choose the best time of day for you to quiet your thoughts and practice silent breathing. This might happen in the morning for some people before the rest of the household gets up. For some, it could be right before bed.

Try finding a peaceful place, closing your eyes, and concentrating on taking deep breaths during whichever time works best for you.

You might check at apps and online meditation choices if you think you could use a little more help.

Practice gratitude

It's quite simple to develop the bad habit of dwelling on your problems, such as the things you detest about your relationship, your life, or your work. Thought cycles like this are something we all occasionally do, they can also occasionally result in depressive symptoms.

Writing down your blessings and practicing thankfulness may help lessen the symptoms of sadness and increase happiness and life satisfaction, according to some study.

Thus, incorporate expressing your gratitude for the things you have every day. They don't have to be substantial items. It may be anything as small as a grin brought on by a butterfly or a kind barista on your way to work.

We all have things for which to be thankful in addition to those for which to be frustrated. It might just take a moment for us to be reminded of it.

Be kind to others

Many of us are prone to concentrating on our own needs and desires, but studies have shown that directing our attention toward supporting others might actually lessen depressive symptoms. Maybe this is because, by reminding us that we are not alone, doing so offers us a sense of purpose that we would not otherwise experience when concentrating only on ourselves.

In any case, attempting to brighten someone else's day is always a good idea. It's not necessary for acts of kindness and compassion to be costly or time-consuming. It might be as easy as holding the door for someone who appears to be carrying a lot or getting a buddy who might be in need of a cup of coffee.

Treat yourself

Self-care is crucial, so do a bit of it while you're at it. Numerous health organizations stress the value of self-care, and research indicates that techniques such as relaxation or meditation may be effective in easing the symptoms of anxiety and depression.

It doesn't hurt to try alternative therapies like aromatherapy, music, or massage even though there isn't much study on them to see if they can improve your mood and help you unwind.

It's not necessary for self-care to be difficult or time-consuming. You may attempt:

- Giving yourself 15 minutes to read a chapter of a book you're enjoying in silence
- Taking bath (warm precisely) or a hot shower at the end of a hard day
- Treating yourself to a face mask will help you relax
- Running around the environment or your neighborhood with your dog

There are no rules here. Simply try choosing at least one activity each day that you know will help you relax or will put a smile on your face.

Wind down

It's no secret that mental health is greatly influenced by the quality of your sleep, so it makes sense to take care of yours by improving your sleep hygiene.

Try starting your nightly ritual at least half an hour before going to bed.

It may be a good idea to begin by shutting off your devices, lowering the lights, and relaxing before your ideally previously established normal bedtime.

When that time arrives, you'll be more likely to be able to fall asleep and remain asleep if you include this into your routine.

When to seek help

No matter how hard you work or how much effort you put into routines and self-care, sadness may still sneak up on you.

Make an effort to remind yourself that depression is a medical illness. Like all other types of sickness, its manifestation is not always within our control.

It might be time to speak with a medical expert or therapist who can help you discover the root of your depression if your symptoms are making it feel hard for you to go about your everyday activities, concentrate, or find joy in things you normally.

CHAPTER 5: PERSONAL NARRATIVES OF HOPE

The journey to overcome depression can be challenging, but with belief in recovery, anything is possible. Although so many patients put much effort in overcoming depression, some still fail to have a permanent healing due to the fact that the type of therapeutic approaches used isn't suitable for the situation of the depressed person which only causes temporary healing.

Reading personal narratives of hope of individuals having overcome depression will let you know that your challenges are not permanent and can be overcome. And this will serve as an insight to learn how different people overcome their depression, their major turning point in recovery, the different things that helped them and lessons learnt from their experiences.

Below are the real-life experiences of people who overcome depression.

Real-life Experiences of Overcoming Depression

Leo's Story

Leo M. Marshall explains how he stopped criticizing himself and how medicine, counseling, and creating a support network helped him get over his depression.

Leo is a mental health advocate and developer of fashion and lifestyle. He is currently creating content for his brand clients, expanding his firm, and campaigning for fair compensation for artists!

Realizing how harshly he was condemning himself for what he saw as a failure to be "normal" was a crucial turning point in his recovery. He wasn't giving himself the grace he was giving to others. He started to relate to his despair better once he gave himself a break.

Some of the things that really helped him

Therapy

He was able to go through the disorganized emotional turmoil in his brain and arrange it into thoughts and ideas with the significant assistance of a therapist.

His support system

After he began helping me with my depression, I contacted several close friends to let them know how I was feeling. It held me responsible, but it also strengthened my friendships with my friends because of my openness.

Medication

Although he was adamantly opposed to taking an antidepressant, he has now realized that it is a tool to aid in his recovery. It's not a phrase. It was a decision, and having some control over his recuperation was tremendously beneficial.

Advice to other people fighting depression

Take a moment to yourself. Never criticize yourself for the things you are unable to feel, do, or express. Talk to others about it as well. It's acceptable to acknowledge when you're having difficulties. Everybody has their ish. You're free to partake in some ish! Those in your life who are aware that you struggle with depression can provide you support.

Jorge's story

The photographer and instructor Jorge E. Greathouse counsels other guys and talks about how he confided in a friend about despair.

A high school instructor who is presently engaged in a picture project on male despair. His intentions are to start this dialogue and raise awareness of this taboo subject.

In actuality, a late-summer night conversation with his closest buddy marked his turning point. He was able to open up to him about how he had been lying to himself for years and that his happiness was only a façade after realizing he was lagging behind in life. "He's the reason why I am here today, thank you CJ" , he remarked.

Some of the things that really helped him

Having a loved one to talk to

It is incredibly helpful to be able to talk to someone you can trust, as he knows it was hard for him to open up to just anyone.

Modifying his diet

Every day when he got home, he would just consume all the junk stuff that was sitting around. His physical and emotional well-being were greatly improved by accepting the shift and encouraging better dietary practices (more vegetables, less carbs).

Accepting himself

For nearly twenty-eight years, he was happy to live in a façade. It was such a relief to be able to let go of that and be himself, and it was a crucial step in helping him discover his fiancé.

Creating art

He said that writing, painting, photography, and other forms of artistic expression are such strong tools for everyone, and even if you don't think you're artistic, you can still release your innermost ideas by writing them down.

Having a dog

It made him want to get out of bed in the mornings to see another living thing that is genuinely delighted to see you every day.

Advice to other people fighting depression

"Don't let prevailing ideas about what it means to be a guy stop you from asking for assistance. Find a loved one who will listen if you don't feel comfortable seeing a therapist. Recognize that I am a genuine person who experienced real depression, and I cannot stress how much better it feels to be free of that darkness. This is not a sponsored script. He said, "Please, put an end to the war you've been fighting for so long. So many men can relate to you."

Dorothy M. Wood

Dorothy M. Wood is twenty-five years old. She writes books. But she had to overcome despair as a youngster to get to where she is now.

Dorothy said that during her adolescence, she was "harassed, humiliated, and cyberbullied," which caused her to change from a joyful and energetic child to someone who was more irate and "sullen." She gradually drifted into the dark waves of sadness when she changed into a new person.

She remarked, "It was the lowest I have ever felt in my life."

But when she enrolled in college, everything was different. She could now finally begin concentrating on what made her distinct and different from the others who had constantly made fun of her and teased her inside the high school walls. She claimed that developing self-confidence was what helped her overcome her sadness and start on the road to success.

Dorothy remarked, "I really tried to change the messages in my head." I was made to feel as though I was repulsive, unattractive, and unworthy. These lessons were absorbed by me, and they shaped who I am now. I started telling myself that I was attractive, intelligent, and adored.

Stephanie P. Scott

Twice in her life, Stephanie battled depression, both times involving death.

The first time was following the death of her sister, and the second was following the birth of her now 12-month-old kid. Her whole family was affected by her sister's passing, but she was particularly affected. She said that it was a sign that nothing lasts forever.

"My priorities for people and events changed after my sister passed away," Stephanie stated in a blog post. "I skimmed the fat from my life and made peace with my own demons."

After that, she got to know Victor, and the two of them had Sharon in 2022. Stephanie too experienced depression after the birth of her daughter. She was depressed more because she had to reassess who she was as a person than because she had a daughter. She was not going to be the party animal she used to be. She needed to take responsibility.

However, Stephanie was soon able to rise beyond her sadness with the assistance of young Sharon.

"My guide is Sharon," Stephanie said on her blog. "My rationale. I left my sales career in February 2023 to work full-time as a life coach because of her. My gut feeling would not go away. And that small voice has my utmost respect. My experiences in life have given me a profound understanding of the underestimated power inherent in our relationships and in our unadulterated human ties.

Additionally, she shared that yoga had assisted her in overcoming her challenges: "Exercise outside is really the secret key to battling depression because it pumps up endorphins, which are needed," she added.

Donald A. Buckley

Donald doesn't talk much about his attempt at suicide or his despair.

Eleven years ago, during his time in college, Farnsworth came dangerously close to taking his own life. However, everything turned around when his roommate discovered him.

He attended college, earned a degree, and presently runs two companies. He expresses gratitude to his friends and family for supporting him in overcoming his sadness.

"I have been able to live a healthy and mostly happy life with the help of my family, many therapists, numerous pharmaceuticals, very good habits, and a lot of time," Donald stated.

Vicki M. Ortego

Vicki M. Ortego, 43, overcame her depression by employing a number of strategies.

Her journey of depression is not over yet. She occasionally has mood swings when she neglects to take care of herself, whether it be with physical or emotional needs.

However, she emerges from the shadows and feels better when she makes use of massage treatment, aromatherapy, and comfort foods. Chapman also avoids going into a sad place by spending her time in more creative and artistic endeavors.

"My depression stays a thing of the past when I use external and internal medicines in a conscious combination," the woman stated.

Jeanne M. Kitchen

Jeanne used to be unable to get out of bed. She was not motivated.

Despite the fact that she seems cheerful and carefree, there was a dramatic shift in her. "I could feel that my hormones were taking me into a very dark place," she added, explaining why she would suddenly start sobbing in the middle of the day.

She tried yoga and exercise, but it didn't really help: she said that she would leave class feeling exhausted and depressed.

How did she then get over her depression? After talking with her nutritionist, she was advised to begin using a natural supplement to assist her hormones balance and steer clear of the more negative feelings.

Sharon S. Galloway

The first time Sharon had depression, she was 57.

Her life took a worse turn when her spouse learned that his previously defeated brain tumor had returned. After his tumor-removal operation, she found it difficult to function and was unable to manage the challenges of helping her husband while also living in a confined space: "I found myself having fits of crying I couldn't stop," she said.

However, how did Sharon get over her depressive state? via writing.

After her husband died, Sharon turned her energies to writing and advancing her profession, which helped her overcome the ghosts that haunted her.

Danny's story

Danny talks about how he overcame his sadness by accepting it rather than pushing it away and how riding a motorcycle gave him freedom.

A 53-year-old husband and father of 3. He loves the great outdoors and riding motorcycles.

He once believed that depression was a condition that only other individuals experienced. that if you put forth enough effort, you might easily get over it. He first made an effort to ignore it. He did a very good job of disguising it from himself, telling himself he was simply feeling a bit low and that it will pass. People familiar with him would never have suspected he was as depressed as he was.

But as time passed, he was unable to get rid of his sense of helplessness and despair. He was growing more and more cut off from the people who had loved him, and he had lost interest in the things he once liked. It was getting harder for him to get the energy to accomplish anything.

While traveling by motorbike in April 2022, he had a significant turning point. He was compelled to take cover in a little hut from an atmospheric occurrence. He was by himself for the next three days and two nights, thinking only to himself. At that moment, he became acutely aware of his depression and the duration of his suffering.

It was the first time he had ever felt completely alone in his life. He was made to face his own inner demons, anxieties, and ideas. It was the first time in his life that he felt really alive, as terrifying as that may seem. He gained the bravery to face his anxieties and work toward a brighter future when he recognized that he had the ability to improve his life.

It had dawned on him that his life was being lived in a robotic autonomous condition. Stand up. Proceed to your job. Return home. Rest. Repeat. He had been living in the past and letting his losses control his present and future, always pursuing the American ideal that had been instilled in him since he was a little boy. Have a successful career, money, a house of your own, a wife, kids, and a dog. Be a decent provider. You are aware of the one. The saying that he discovered redemption on the back of a motorcycle may seem corny, but it's real. He's in charge of his motorcycle. It's thrilling to be able to forge his own path.

He's beginning to realize that, although his melancholy and social anxiety are beyond his control, they are still something he can manage. He now understands that life is a valuable gift and that it is worthwhile to live. There are always going to be obstacles and disappointments, but there is also happiness and beauty. He's rediscovering how to be content in the here and now and to enjoy the little things in life. He is aware that it won't be simple and that there will be days when it seems to drag on forever, but he also knows that there is hope and that there are people who care.

Some of the things that really helped him

- His motorbike rides have always been beneficial.
- discussing his mental health with pals.
- putting forth the time to thoughtfully examine and contemplate.
- requesting medical guidance.

Advice to other people fighting depression

"I would start by assuring them that they are not alone. I would then advise them to talk to friends and relatives about what they're going through. In addition, I would listen to their opinions and point them in the direction of useful information," he stated.

Lessons Gained from Personal Journeys

- Working with a therapist plays a huge role in recovery.
- Having people's support; parents, family and friends who are ready to listen, talk and stay with you through the difficult phase.
- Medication is also a tool to support recovery.
- Judging yourself on things you can't do or feel won't help your case.
- Accepting who you are and reminding yourself consistently.
- Changing diet and promoting healthier eating habits can help your physical and mental state.
- Having another living being that is just so excited to see you exist everyday is a motivation e.g child, pet e.t.c
- Exercises like yoga will aid you in your recovery process.
- Writing about how your day goes, the actions you took and how you feel about then is also a good idea.
- Lastly, taking the time to really look inside and reflect goes a long way.

CHAPTER 6: TOOLS FOR TRANSFORMATION

Tools for Transformation" represents a compass guiding individuals through the intricate terrain of overcoming depression. In this multifaceted section, a set of practical and empowering tools are introduced, designed to initiate positive change and foster personal growth. Journaling prompts serve as a contemplative avenue, encouraging individuals to delve into their thoughts and emotions. This reflective practice not only aids in self-discovery but also becomes a means of expression, allowing individuals to navigate and make sense of the intricate labyrinth of their emotions.

The focus is on mindfulness exercises as an effective means of developing awareness in the present moment. Through mindfulness exercises, people become more aware of the present moment, which promotes composure and resilience in the face of adversity. These activities serve as anchors, bringing people back to the present and providing a haven from the frequently turbulent waves of depressing thoughts and feelings.

Setting goals becomes evident as a transformative toolkit's beacon of deliberate change. This instrument functions as a rehabilitation road map by motivating users to create reasonable and doable objectives. These objectives provide as concrete markers of advancement as well as milestones, encouraging a feeling of agency and direction. "Tools for Transformation" encompasses an ever-changing range of materials, encouraging people to actively shape their journey toward well-being, one reflective journal entry, mindful breath, and intentional goal at a time.

Practical Exercises for Self-Reflection

Meditate: Because it gives us the opportunity to stop and think, meditation is a great tool for introspection.

Keep a Journal: Writing down your thoughts, feelings, and life experiences in a journal allows you to preserve a lasting record of them. You'll be able to reflect on your earlier ideas and experiences thanks to this.

Talk to yourself: When you talk to yourself, you're forced to express your feelings in a way that makes sense to you at the moment. If you're unsure, pay attention to the words you use to yourself. Jot down or document your feelings as the day draws closer, you make choices, and you engage with others.

Possessing a unique vision: One way to do this is to focus on your objectives while working out. Discuss your objectives with a personal trainer or take some time to consider your current situation.

Develop routines and practice often: By purposefully practicing self-reflection, you may ask insightful questions, analyze your own experiences, and weigh the effects of your choices.

Strengths analysis: One discovers a method via the power of observation and introspection. Thus, one must always explore deeper and deeper.

Write morning pages. It's great for problem solving, generating ideas, and calming fears. Take a piece of paper as soon as you wake up and write down anything that comes to mind. You want to clear your thoughts, therefore don't filter anything.

Challenge your beliefs: Consider a cause that you are very passionate about. It may be about the people in your life, the environment, or yourself. Consider your reasons for holding this idea and the events or sources of inspiration that shaped it.

Understanding the origins of your views is one of the enlightening aspects of this phase. Then imagine if your belief were to be proven to be false. What behavioral or attitudinal changes would that bring about? Although it might be difficult, this is the phase where the magic happens. It all comes down to taking a risk and adopting a fresh perspective on the world.

Make a bucket list: Making a bucket list is a morbid yet eye-opening practice. A bucket list is more than just once-in-a-lifetime experiences like skydiving or bungee jumping, even though many individuals include these things. One may include forgiving someone who has wronged them in the past or falling in love as goals. Think about what these items on your bucket list say about you and the kind of life you want to lead as you write them down.

Mindfulness meditation: Mindfulness means being aware without passing judgment. You may be aware of what's going on inside of you or of your environment. As you become more self-aware, you will be able to identify when tension is building up in your body or when emotions like grief, rage, or irritation are starting to surface. You can manage your environment and take proper action when you foresee uncontrollably high levels of stress by practicing mindfulness meditation.

Name your emotions: Give your emotions a name. Increasing the range of emotions in your vocabulary will help you express yourself more clearly.

Observing others: We can watch others to attempt to understand them, just as we can use our body to convey how we want other people to see us.

Practice breathing techniques: Breathing techniques, like meditation, can improve your ability to think effectively. You can practice self-reflection by breathing in deeply with your nose and out slowly and rhythmically through your lips.

Reflect on past decisions: You need to establish calm and relaxation in order to interact with your inner self. We can only examine our history and future in this manner, evaluating our errors and pinpointing areas in which we still need to grow. You should thus schedule times specifically for unwinding and spending time with yourself.

Take a long walk: Going on a long walk is a terrific way to clear your mind. A lengthy stroll may help you reflect on your motivations, your beliefs, concerns and fears, and much more. While high-intensity exercises like running or HIIT workouts might be beneficial when you're overthinking, walking can help you reflect on much more.

Mindfulness Techniques for Healing

One of the most important components in enabling improvement in emotional and mental health is mindfulness. Mindfulness treatments, with its components of awareness, attention, and consciousness, have been repeatedly linked to a range of emotional wellness metrics.

When you practice mindfulness meditation, you concentrate on paying close attention to your senses and emotions in the present moment, without giving it any meaning or passing judgment. Using breathing techniques, guided imagery, and other techniques to calm the body and mind and lessen stress are all part of the mindfulness practice.

Furthermore, mindfulness training has been demonstrated to have measurable results in relaxation, which is beneficial for diseases associated to stress and the physiological reactions they cause. But mindfulness is more than a method of relaxation. It is regarded as a type of mental training that lessens the sensitivity to thoughts. Although relaxation may result from this, the benefits go much beyond simple stress relief.

Mindfulness techniques for healing include the following exercises:

Breathing exercises

Because the breath is an experience that may be focused on in the present moment and is a constant aspect of life, mindful breathing exercises are especially effective. The sympathetic and parasympathetic nervous systems are directly correlated with breathing, which can contribute to other elements of relaxation and stress reduction.

The goal of mindful breathing is to get the client to sit in a comfortable posture, either with their eyes open or closed, and to focus on their breathing sensations. Ask them to just observe the characteristics of the breath with curiosity and without passing judgment.

- Is it swift or sluggish, shallow or deep?
- They notice feelings in the body?
- Do they see the breath in the stomach, rib cage, nose, or back of the throat?

As their attention wanders, have them notice it and bring their attention gently back to the breath

Body scan meditation

A full body scan meditation takes thirty to forty-five minutes. Stress and tension can be released by having the client just notice with awareness as this mindfulness technique focuses attention on the body without passing judgment (especially on aches, pains, tightness, or tension).

Body scan meditations come in a variety of forms, but often include the practitioner having the client lie on their back in a comfortable posture with their legs apart and their arms at their sides, with their palms facing up (a receiving gesture). Body parts will be noticed by the client in a methodical manner, beginning with the toes.

They may be instructed to check their feelings, take note of the temperature, release tension, and focus their breath on their toes. Body part by body part (ankle, calf, knee, thigh, etc.) on one side, the scan will advance upward before switching to the other.

After each bodily component has been scanned, it is combined, and the emphasis changes to how they are all connected. Seeing the body as a whole, connected by the movement of breath in and out, is one of the goals of the body scan.

Guided imagery

Through a variety of signals, guided imagery guides people through relaxation techniques and allows them to explore visual images. To aid with relaxing, pleasant imagery—like a stunning location—is frequently used. The individual experiencing the imagery controls it, regardless of whether the client or the doctor generates the image or presents the notion.

Guided imagery induces altered states of awareness and gives one a sensation of control and mastery. Through communication with the subconscious, this technique helps people detach from pain, suffering, and tension.

The practitioner is encouraged via guided imagery to be as creative and detailed as they can, utilizing all of their senses. It's crucial to pay attention to any ideas, feelings, and even physical repercussions that surface during guided imagery.

Mindful eating

Eating with awareness involves being aware of the smell, taste, chewing, and swallowing sensations of the meal. This is known as mindful eating. It is focusing attention on eating without passing judgment in the here and now, minute by moment.

Although it may be done with any meal, mindful eating is typically done with something straightforward, like a slice of orange. The orange slice's color, texture, fragrance, and feel are to be noted by the client. After that, students take a single bite and observe how the flavor and feelings alter as they chew and swallow the orange. It is important to perform the exercise slowly, deliberately, and thoughtfully.

A person's connection with food may be improved and eating disorders and body image can be addressed via mindful eating. It can also foster a greater appreciation for meals and the nourishing effects they have on our bodies and lives.

CHAPTER 7: NAVIGATING DARK MOMENTS

Navigating dark moments is a profound journey that requires resilience, introspection, and a compassionate understanding of one's own emotional landscape. In these challenging times, individuals often find themselves in the throes of intense emotions, grappling with the shadows that cast a veil over their well-being. The process of navigating darkness involves acknowledging the depth of one's feelings, allowing space for vulnerability, and seeking support when needed. It's a courageous expedition into the unknown, where each step may feel heavy, yet each step forward is an act of strength and endurance.

During these moments of darkness, self-reflection becomes a guiding compass. Individuals navigate the contours of their thoughts and emotions, seeking to understand the roots of their struggles. It's a delicate dance between confronting discomfort and embracing self-compassion. Navigating dark moments is not about evading the shadows but rather about finding a path through them. With time, resilience, and the support of others, individuals can emerge from these challenging moments with a newfound understanding of themselves and a heightened ability to face future adversities with courage and insight.

Coping Strategies for Setbacks

Definition of setbacks

Setbacks are impediments or difficulties that impede our advancement or result in a brief relapse in our mental health journey. These failures can be caused by a variety of things, including unanticipated life events, external stresses, or emotional triggers.

The emotional toll of setbacks

A variety of feelings, such as annoyance, disappointment, melancholy, and even hopelessness, might arise from encountering setbacks. It's critical to recognize and accept these feelings while actively looking for coping mechanisms.

There are two types of coping mechanisms for setbacks.

- **Embracing Resilience**: Strategies for Bouncing Back
- **Moving Forward**: Maintaining Progress

Although failures are a part of life, you have the ability to view them as teaching opportunities rather than as discouraging setbacks. Gaining the ability to overcome difficulties and failures can help you advance and accomplish your objectives.

Building Resilience in the Face of Challenges

Embracing Resilience: Strategies for Bouncing Back

Cultivating self-compassion

Self-compassion is resilience's cornerstone. When you have setbacks, be gentle, compassionate, and patient with yourself. Engage in constructive self-talk, confront self-defeating ideas, and keep in mind that obstacles are just momentary side trips rather than permanent barriers.

Seeking support

Make use of your support system when things get tough. This can include dependable family members, friends, or medical experts like counselors or therapists. Talking to people about your feelings and ideas might help you gain perspective, direction, and comfort.

Reflecting on progress

Consider how far along you've gone in terms of your mental wellness. Remind yourself of the progress you've made and celebrate your successes. This self-reflection might help you become motivated again and boost your self-assurance that you can get beyond obstacles.

Developing coping mechanisms

Find healthy coping strategies that suit your needs. Take part in things that make you happy, calm down, or feel fulfilled. Exercise, writing, mindfulness exercises, creating art, and spending time in nature are a few examples of this. Discovering constructive outlets can make overcoming obstacles easier.

Setting realistic goals

In difficult circumstances, it's critical to review and modify your objectives. Establish reasonable expectations that are in line with your present situation. Divide more ambitious objectives into more manageable chunks so that you may feel accomplished as you go.

Moving Forward: Maintaining Progress

Learning from setbacks

Failures provide important chances for development and introspection. Analyze the circumstances surrounding the setback and look for any trends or triggers. Make use of this understanding to create plans for averting future disappointments and enhancing your ability to bounce back.

Practicing self-care

Make self-care a priority since it's essential to sustaining your development. This entails obtaining adequate rest, feeding your body a balanced diet, and partaking in rejuvenating and relaxing activities. Self-care promotes your mental health journey and improves your general well-being.

Building a support system

Be in the company of positive and inspiring people. Develop connections with others who empathize with your struggles and offer unwavering assistance. Having a solid support network can help you overcome obstacles by providing accountability and encouragement.

Engaging in therapy or counseling

Think about contacting mental health specialists such as therapists or counselors for expert assistance. These experts can offer direction, coping mechanisms, and individualized help catered to your particular need. Counseling or therapy can be a very helpful tool for you to overcome obstacles and keep moving forward.

CHAPTER 8: Embracing Light: A Journey to Healing

This transformative odyssey encourages individuals to step into the warmth of illumination amid life's challenges. This narrative is a celebration of resilience, hope, and the innate capacity for growth that resides within every individual. In the face of adversity, embracing light becomes a conscious choice—a commitment to seeking out the positive, the uplifting, and the transformative aspects of one's journey. It is a call to acknowledge that even in the darkest moments, there exists a potential for healing and renewal.

The journey of "Embracing Light" is multifaceted, encompassing self-discovery, self-compassion, and the cultivation of a positive mindset. It encourages individuals to explore their strengths, confront their vulnerabilities, and find solace in the luminous moments that illuminate their path. It also urges individuals to recognize that healing is not a linear process but a dynamic and evolving experience. Through embracing light, individuals not only navigate their struggles but also foster a sense of empowerment, guiding them towards a space where healing becomes an active and transformative force in their lives.

Sustainable Practices for Continued Mental Wellness

Mindful Practices: Incorporate mindfulness and meditation into your daily routine to promote emotional well-being and stress reduction.

Regular Exercise: Establish a consistent exercise routine, engaging in activities that you enjoy for physical and mental health benefits.

Balanced Nutrition: Maintain a balanced and nutritious diet, emphasizing whole foods that contribute to overall well-being.

Adequate Sleep: Prioritize consistent and sufficient sleep to support cognitive function and emotional resilience.

Social Connections: Cultivate and nurture meaningful relationships, fostering a supportive social network.

Nature Exposure: Spend time in nature regularly, as it has been linked to improved mood and reduced stress levels.

Stress Management Techniques: Develop and practice stress management techniques, such as deep breathing, progressive muscle relaxation, or yoga.

Limiting Screen Time: Set boundaries on screen time to promote a healthy balance and reduce potential negative impacts on mental health.

Time Management: Implement effective time management strategies to reduce stress and enhance productivity.

Continuous Learning: Engage in ongoing learning and personal development to stimulate the mind and maintain a sense of purpose.

Fostering Supportive Environments

It is estimated that millions of individuals worldwide suffer from mental health disorders. Significant harm has been done to mental health as a result of the COVID-19 epidemic, with anxiety, depression, and other issues rising. It is therefore more crucial than ever to create a setting that supports mental wellness.

A welcoming atmosphere helps lessen the stigma associated with mental illness and facilitate people's access to care. It can enhance people's general well-being by encouraging healthy coping strategies and lowering stress levels. Moreover, a nurturing atmosphere might result in higher output and involvement in the community, school, or business.

Ways to build a supportive environment for mental health

Educate and Increase Awareness

Creating awareness and education is one of the most important methods to create a supportive atmosphere for mental health. Teaching people about mental health entails educating them about the symptoms and warning signs of mental health issues, the value of getting treatment, and easily available resources.

Education programs that attempt to lessen the stigma attached to mental illness can be beneficial for communities, businesses, and schools. Workshops, seminars, and training sessions might be included in these programs. Making educational resources like pamphlets, posters, and brochures is another method to increase public awareness of mental health concerns.

Using social media sites like Facebook, Twitter, and Instagram to provide resources and information on mental health is another approach to raise awareness. This makes it easier for people to talk about mental health problems and ask for assistance when they do.

Encourage Open Communication

Establishing an atmosphere that promotes mental wellness requires open communication. Promoting an accepting environment where individuals may discuss mental health issues without fear of stigma or condemnation is crucial.

One-on-one meetings, team-building exercises, and frequent check-ins can all help to foster open communication. It's also essential to have open channels of communication, such a mental health hotline, counseling service, or employee help program.

Leaders may act as role models for others and inspire others to take similar actions by being transparent about their personal difficulties with mental health. This can lessen the stigma attached to mental health and promote a culture of understanding and support.

Provide Resources and Support

The availability of resources and assistance is a crucial component in creating a setting that supports mental health. Resources include things like support groups, mental health programs, and counseling services. To assist individuals in managing their mental health, employers and educators might provide flexible work schedules or mental health days.

It's critical to have a support system in place for those who might be struggling with mental health concerns. This might be an employee aid program, mental health support services, or therapy. People who have a network of support will feel less isolated and more taken care of.

Encouraging Work-Life Balance

Supporting work-life balance is another useful strategy to establish a culture that is conducive to mental wellness. Stress at work causes many people to suffer from mental health issues, which can result in burnout, anxiety, and depression. People can better control their stress levels and preserve excellent mental health by encouraging work-life balance.

For instance, employers could provide remote work choices, mental health days, or flexible working hours. Extracurricular activities that encourage interaction with others, physical activity, and creativity can be offered by schools. Communities may host occasions or initiatives that encourage rest and self-care.

APPENDIX

Mental Health Organizations and Helplines

List of Mental Health Organizations

National Alliance on Mental Illness (NAMI):
Helpline: 1-800-950-NAMI (6264)

Mental Health America (MHA):
Helpline: 1-800-273-TALK (1-800-273-8255)

World Health Organization (WHO) - Mental Health:
No specific helpline; refer to local mental health services.

The Jed Foundation:
Helpline: Text "HELLO" to 741741

American Foundation for Suicide Prevention (AFSP):
Helpline: 1-800-273-TALK (1-800-273-8255)

Mind (UK):
Infoline: 0300 123 3393

Beyond Blue (Australia):

Helpline: 1300 22 4636

Canadian Mental Health Association (CMHA):

Refer to local CMHA branches for specific helpline numbers.

Sane Australia:

Helpline: 1800 187 263

To Write Love on Her Arms (TWLOHA):

Helpline: Text "TWLOHA" to 741741

Other mental Organizations and Their helplines

United States

- 988 Mental Health Emergency Hotline: In July 2022, a universal mental health crisis line launched nationwide. Calling 988 will connect you to a crisis counselor regardless of where you are in the United States.
- 911 Emergency
- National Alliance on Mental Illness (NAMI) HelpLine: 1-800-950-NAMI, or text "HELPLINE" to 62640. Both services available between 10 a.m. and 10 p.m. ET, Monday–Friday
- In October 2023 NAMI launched a Teen & Young Adult HelpLine, for nation-wide peer support and resource referrals. Text "Friend" to 62640; chat at nami.org/talktous; call 800-950-6264. Available Mondays through Fridays, 10 a.m. to 10 p.m. ET.
- National Domestic Violence Hotline: 1-800-799-7233
- National Suicide Prevention Lifeline: 1-800-273-TALK (8255); www.suicidepreventionlifeline.org. Or, just dial 988
- Suicide Prevention, Awareness, and Support: www.suicide.org

- Crisis Text Line: Text REASON to 741741 (free, confidential and 24/7). In English and Spanish
- Self-Harm Hotline: 1-800-DONT CUT (1-800-366-8288)
- Family Violence Helpline: 1-800-996-6228
- Planned Parenthood Hotline: 1-800-230-PLAN (7526)
- American Association of Poison Control Centers: 1-800-222-1222
- National Council on Alcoholism & Drug Dependency: 1-800-622-2255
- LGBTQ Hotline: 1-888-843-4564
- National Maternal Mental Health Hotline: 1-833-TLC-MAMA (1-833-852-6262)
- The Trevor Project: 1-866-488-7386 or text "START" to 678678. Standard text messaging rates apply. Available 24/7/365. (Provides crisis intervention and suicide prevention services to lesbian, gay, bisexual, transgender, queer & questioning—LGBTQ—young people under 25.)
- The SAGE LGBT Elder Hotline connects LGBT older people and caretakers with friendly responders. 1-877-360-LGBT (5428)
- The Trans Lifeline is staffed by transgender people for transgender people:
- 1-877-565-8860 (United States)
- 1-877-330-6366 (Canada)
- Rape Abuse and Incest National Network (RAINN) is the nation's largest organization fighting sexual violence: (800) 656-HOPE / (800) 810-7440 (TTY)
- Veterans Crisis Line: https://www.veteranscrisisline.net
- International Suicide Prevention Directory: findahelpline.com
- The StrongHearts Native Helpline is a confidential and anonymous culturally appropriate domestic violence and dating violence helpline for Native Americans, available every day from 7 a.m. to 10 p.m. CT. Call 1-844-762-8483.

Canada

- Emergency: 911
- Hotline: 1-888-353-2273

- YourLifeCounts.org: https://yourlifecounts.org/find-help/

UK & Republic of Ireland

- Emergency: 112 or 999
- Hotline: +44 (0) 8457 90 90 90 (UK - local rate)
- Hotline: +44 (0) 8457 90 91 92 (UK minicom)
- Hotline: 1850 60 90 90 (ROI - local rate)
- Hotline: 1850 60 90 91 (ROI minicom)
- YourLifeCounts.org: https://yourlifecounts.org/find-help/

Argentina

- Emergency: 911
- Recuerde siempre que si usted esta en una situación de emergencia debe comunicarse con los teléfonos: *107 (SAME-Sistema de Atención Medica de Emergencia), *911 (Emergencia policial), para atención telefónica inmediata. Si desea orientación telefónica a familiares y amigos, déjenos su mensaje y teléfono. Nos comunicaremos con usted.

Spain

- Emergency: 112
- Telefono De La Esperanza - 963916006 - http://telefonodelaesperanza.org

Australia

- Emergency: 000

- Lifeline.org: https://www.lifeline.org.au/Get-Help/Online-Services/crisis-chat
- LifeLine Australia: 1-300-13-11-14
- YourLifeCounts.org: https://yourlifecounts.org/find-help/

South Africa

- Emergency: 10 111 for police or 10 177 for an ambulance
- 24hr Helpline: 0800 12 13 14 or SMS 31393 (and we will call you back)
- Depression and Anxiety Helpline: 0800 70 80 90
- YourLifeCounts.org: https://yourlifecounts.org/find-help/

New Zealand

- Emergency: 111
- Lifeline 24/7 Helpline: 0800 543 354
- Suicide Crisis Helpline: 0508 828 865 (0508 TAUTOKO)
- YourLifeCounts.org: https://yourlifecounts.org/find-help/

Germany

- Emergency: 112
- Hotline: 800 111 0111
- Hotline: 0800 111 0222
- YourLifeCounts.org: https://yourlifecounts.org/find-help/

France

- SOS Help

- Boite Postale 43,
- Cedex 92101
- Boulogne
- Hotline: 01 46 21 46 46
- Website: soshelpline.org (English-speaking)
- Suicide Ecoute

Paris

- Hotline: 01 45 39 40 00
- Website: suicide.ecoute.free.fr
- E.P.E. idF. Fil Sante Jeunes
- Paris
- Hotline: 0800 235 236
- Website: filsantejeunes.com
- Fédération S.O.S Amitié France
- 11, rue des Immeubles industriels
- 75011Paris
- Hotline: (+33) (0)1 40 09 15 22
- Website: sos-amitie.com

Italy

- Samaritans - ONLUS
- Via San Giovanni in Laterano 250
- 00184
- ROME
- Hotline: 800 86 00 22
- Website: http://www.samaritansonlus.org
- Telefono Amico Italia
- CP 337

- 38100
- Trento
- Hotline: 199 284 284
- Website: telefonoamico.it

Serbia

- SRCE Novi Sad
- NOVI SAD
- Hotline: 0800-300-303
- Website: https://www.centarsrce.org/index.php
- E-mail Helpline: vanja@centarsrce.org

Mexico

- Mexico Suicide Hotline: 5255102550

Japan

- Befrienders Worldwide, Tokyo
- Hotline: +81 (0) 3 5286 9090
- Website: https://www.befrienders-jpn.org
- BI Suicide Prevention Centre, Osaka
- Hotline: +81 (0) 6 4395 4343
- Website: spc-osaka.org
- Tokyo English Lifeline / TELL Japan
- 5-4 22 rm 302, Minami Aoyama
- Minao Ku
- Hotline: Counselling: 03 5774 0992
- Hotline: Face to Face: 03 3498 0231

- Website: https://telljp.com

Brazil

- AMA National Association
- 90035191
- Hospital de Pronto Socorro de Porto Alegre
- Largo Teodoro Herzl, s/nº - Bom Fim, Porto Alegre - RS, 90040-192, Brazil
- CVV Sao Paulo – National Association
- 55 11 31514109
- Website: cvv.org.br
- Sociedade de Amigos Voluntarios
- Hotline: (19) 3231-4111
- https://sociedadeamigosdavida.org.br

India

- AASRA
- 91-9820466726
- Available 24 hours, 7 days a week, in English and Hindi
- http://www.aasra.info/helpline.html